Editorial Project Management

Second edition

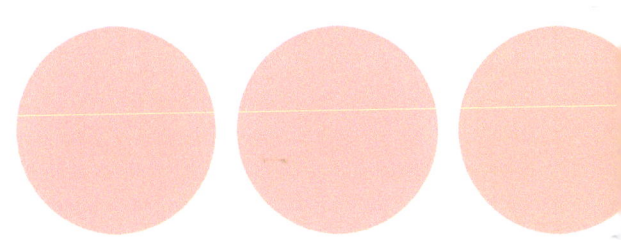

Abi Saffrey
with Emily Kopieczek

First published in the UK in 2024 by
Chartered Institute of Editing and Proofreading
Studio 206, Milton Keynes Business Centre
Foxhunter Drive, Linford Wood
Milton Keynes
Buckinghamshire
MK14 6GD

ciep.uk

Copyright © 2024 Chartered Institute of Editing and Proofreading

ISBN 978 1 915141 34 7 (print)
ISBN 978 1 915141 33 0 (PDF ebook)
ISBN 978 1 915141 35 4 (ePub)

Second edition

First edition 2019, ISBN 978 1 9161481 0 9 (print) and 978 1 9161481 1 6 (ebook)

All rights reserved. No part of this publication may be reproduced or used in any manner without written permission from the publisher, except for quoting brief passages in a review.

The moral rights of the authors have been asserted.

The information in this work is accurate and current at the time of publication to the best of the author's and publisher's knowledge, but it has been written as a short summary or introduction only. Readers are advised to take further steps to ensure the correctness, sufficiency or completeness of this information for their own purposes.

Typeset in-house
Original design by Ave Design (**avedesign.studio**)
Image credits: Pixabay and Shutterstock

Contents

1 |	Glossary	1
2 |	Introduction	3
3 |	What is editorial project management?	5
4 |	What is a project?	10
	An editorial project	10
5 |	Scheduling	13
	Critical paths	13
	Things to consider when creating a schedule	15
	Scheduling tools and presentation	17
	Managing a schedule	18
	Dealing with the unexpected	21
	Scheduling your own time	22
6 |	Briefing	23
	Understanding the client's brief	23
	Briefing your team	24
	Briefing a wide range of suppliers and team members	25
7 |	Budgeting	26
	Setting the budget	26

| 8 | Management and communication | 32 |

Selecting the right people 32
Working with your client 34
Reporting and feedback 34
Keep calm and carry on 36

| 9 | Working for a project management company | 38 |

Project set up 38
Communication 38
Schedule 39
Budget 40

| 10 | Being an editorial project manager | 41 |

Communication 41
Managing your own time 43
Keeping records 43
Building up and using the experience 45

| 11 | Resources | 46 |

1 | Glossary

Editorial project management comes with a wide array of jargon: most of the terminology relates to simple and clearly defined tasks and processes but knowing some key words and phrases can boost confidence.

This list is by no means exhaustive – as well as publishing-specific terms, there are many different project management approaches with their own terminology.

1PP, 2PP, 3PP – First proofs, second proofs, third proofs (always in capitals to distinguish from 'pp' used for page ranges, eg 'pp96–105')

agile – a style of project management (originating from software development) focusing on continuous improvement and flexibility

budget – the money assigned to a project and how it is allocated

critical path – the order of the main tasks that must be undertaken to complete a project

deliverables – physical or digital items to be produced (such as proofs)

dependencies – the relationship between items where the completion of one is dependent on the completion (or progress) of another

extent – number of pages in a book (usually in multiples of four or eight, due to printing processes)

Gantt chart – a bar chart that shows the durations of stages within a project and any overlaps and/or dependencies

issue – something unexpected that happens and needs to be managed (this may be recorded in an issue log)

kanban board – a visual workflow tool with multiple columns (can be digital or physical – often with sticky notes)

kick-off meeting – the initial meeting at the start of the project bringing together stakeholders and the project manager(s)

life cycle – all stages of a project from the initial planning phase through to the final outcome (eg the sales of a published book)

milestones – key points in the schedule

packager – an organisation offering end-to-end publishing services, including project management. They will often work on behalf of a publisher to oversee a project from beginning to end

process – encapsulates all the tasks and activities involved in a project

RAG – red, amber, green status – used to show how a project (or a stage within it) is going

retrospective meeting – a meeting held at the end of the project to review what went well and what could have gone better, usually looking at areas including budget, schedule, suppliers and quality. The outcomes of the meeting can inform the planning of future projects

risk – something that can be planned for (and hopefully avoided)

schedule – a timeline for the tasks in the project

scope – a detailed breakdown of what the project is

scope creep – changes, continuous or uncontrolled growth in a project's scope, at any point after the project begins

stakeholder – someone who has a stake in a project, but is not necessarily involved in its creation (such as those working in sales and marketing)

video conferencing – software suites such as Zoom and Microsoft Teams, which are increasingly popular for team meetings in an editorial project management context

workflow – the specific sequence of tasks involved in taking a project from beginning to end

2 | Introduction

This guide is for you if you:

- want to know what editorial project management is
- are thinking about adding editorial project management to your skillset
- are considering taking on editorial project management responsibilities.

You may currently be:

- a copyeditor
- a proofreader
- a typesetter
- an editorial assistant
- an administrator within an organisation that creates publications
- someone with an interest in the publishing process.

This guide will introduce you to the key concepts of editorial project management, and get you thinking about what skills and knowledge are required.

Bear in mind that every project is different, and that includes the terminology (including job titles), tasks, people, content, processes, workflows and end results. It isn't possible in this short guide to provide definitive details of what a project looks like or what you may be expected to do as there are many variables – and an editorial project manager needs to be able to adapt to different ways of working.

This guide will not turn you into an efficient, thorough and competent editorial project manager – further training and experience will. A good place to start is the CIEP's online course **Editorial Project Management**, which provides detailed study notes around each topic and uses case studies and exercises to deepen understanding.

3 | What is editorial project management?

Project management

Before looking at editorial project management, let's step back and look at the wider concept of project management.

> ### Some definitions
> - Project management is the application of processes, methods, knowledge, skills and experience to achieve the project objectives.
> - Project management is the discipline of initiating, planning, executing, controlling and closing the work of a team to achieve specific goals and meet specific success criteria.

These are definitions of project management using project management jargon. To put it more simply, project management is controlling the process of making a product. There are many different project management methodologies, including PRINCE2, agile, critical path and extreme – these will be mentioned briefly where relevant in this guide. You may wish to do some research to find a working method that suits you.

Editorial project management

Editorial project management is about getting content published – making it happen. Content (text, images, figures, tables) goes from a raw, draft form, through quality control and production processes, to a finished product.

The finished product may be:

- a website or blog
- printed books, both fiction and non-fiction
- journals, magazines or pamphlets
- online learning materials
- company reports or corporate literature
- newsletters for an organisation
- information sheets
- brochures, leaflets, flyers or advertising and marketing materials
- conference proceedings
- guidelines, protocols and best practice
- any other document published in printed or digital formats.

An editorial project manager:

- plans
- commissions suppliers (and provides them with constructive feedback)
- manages the budget
- manages the schedule
- monitors quality
- manages risks and changes

3 | What is editorial project management?

- ensures the project is completed (ideally on time and within the budget)
- evaluates and reports back on the success of the project.

An editorial project is:

- temporary – with a finite and definite timescale; once it is complete, those who have worked on it will move on to other projects
- unique – it may be similar to other projects, but will have its own scope, requirements and quirks
- cross-functional – people from different teams with different specialisms will work on the project, and the editorial project manager has to bring them and the needs of the project together.

Becoming an editorial project manager

There isn't one perfect route to becoming an editorial project manager – you need the skills, determination and a willingness to learn and adapt.

Routes into project management*

Tessa had worked as a freelance copyeditor for publishers for a few years, when a couple of those clients asked her to take on some project management work, and those clients provided the support and guidance she needed to build on her existing skills.

Arek began his editing career with a small business-to-business publisher, working in-house with three other editors. His manager noticed that Arek was good at prioritising his workload and had shown an interest in the wider publishing process, so asked him to lead the creation and production of a new publication. Arek took the CIEP's and the Publishing Training Centre's (PTC) Editorial Project Management courses when he started his own business, so that he was able to offer project management services alongside editing and proofreading.

* Real scenarios but names changed

Your background and current post may not explicitly feature project management, but they may well have given you the essential 'soft skills':

- communication
- diplomacy
- cooperation
- delegation
- the ability to quickly adapt and learn
- time management
- organisation
- resilience
- the ability to prioritise.

These soft skills can enable those with the necessary technical skills to do their job within the publication process. You may have those skills from your current role, or you may use them in your non-work life (as a volunteer, a carer, a homeowner). Reflect on what you do and how you do it to help you identify whether project management is for you, and if there are any skills you need to develop or hone.

When does editorial project management start?

Before an editorial project manager gets involved
In traditional book publishing, projects begin when a commissioning editor or publisher identifies a need for a book on a specific topic in a specific style. An author may have approached them with an idea, or the publisher may approach a potential author. The publisher (or product owner) will work with the author to ensure the content meets the agreed requirements. The product owner is likely to work with designers and the production department to get an idea of what the finished book will look like, as well as agreeing on the print run (if applicable), the budget and the publication date.

Other content – both digital and print – may well follow a similar process, with a product owner identifying a need, making decisions about who will create what content, and the relevant timeframes and costs.

An editorial project manager's involvement
In a book-publishing environment, the editorial project manager will have a handover (or transmittal or kick-off) meeting with the product owner and production team (perhaps also the design team or digital specialists), at which point they become the lead for the publishing stages that follow. Face-to-face meetings are ideal, as meeting in person builds connections which help improve communication across the life cycle of a project. However, given that project teams are becoming increasingly international, online meetings using tools such as Zoom or Microsoft Teams are fast becoming the norm. Online meetings offer greater flexibility and have distinct advantages:

- They encourage better turn-taking, allowing all participants a chance to express themselves without interruption.
- The software comes with a host of useful features, such as screen sharing and muting.
- The meetings can be recorded – it can be very useful to have the kick-off meeting to refer back to.

The editorial project manager's involvement is likely to end once the final files are signed off by all stakeholders, and passed to the production team for printing and/or digital publication. This may also be the case in the workflow and processes for other content, depending on the needs of the organisation and the type of content.

Every organisation will use different processes and workflows (see **An editorial project** for more on these), so editorial project managers need to be flexible and adaptable.

4 | What is a project?

Before going into more detail about what editorial project management involves, it's essential to think about what a 'project' is.

At the beginning of every project, the product owner (an individual, a team, a department) will need to answer the following questions:

- What is the market/who is the audience?
- What is the medium?
- What is the scope?
- What is the budget?
- What is the timescale?

The answers to these questions will define what the finished product needs to be, and the processes and people involved in creating that finished product.

The product owner may also be the writer, the illustrator, the designer and/or the editorial project manager – it depends on the structure and processes used by the publishing organisation.

An editorial project

As covered in the previous chapter, a project in this context involves turning draft content into a published product, in a printed or digital format.

Draft content needs to go through a range of quality control and production processes, which turn it into something polished and presentable. The key terms here are **process** and **workflow**. These are closely related and it's hard to find clear definitions that aren't in business

4 | What is a project?

speak (steer clear of business forum discussions about the differences or you may find yourself falling down a rabbit hole …). By and large, **process** tends to be used as a wider term: 'the publishing process', encapsulating all the tasks and activities involved. The workflow is the specific sequence of tasks that takes a project from beginning to end.

Below is the workflow for the publication of a first edition of a typical CIEP guide, at the time of writing.

No two organisations will use the same workflow, though those used by different book publishers may be very similar. Some organisations may not have a tried and tested workflow in place, or may have no idea where

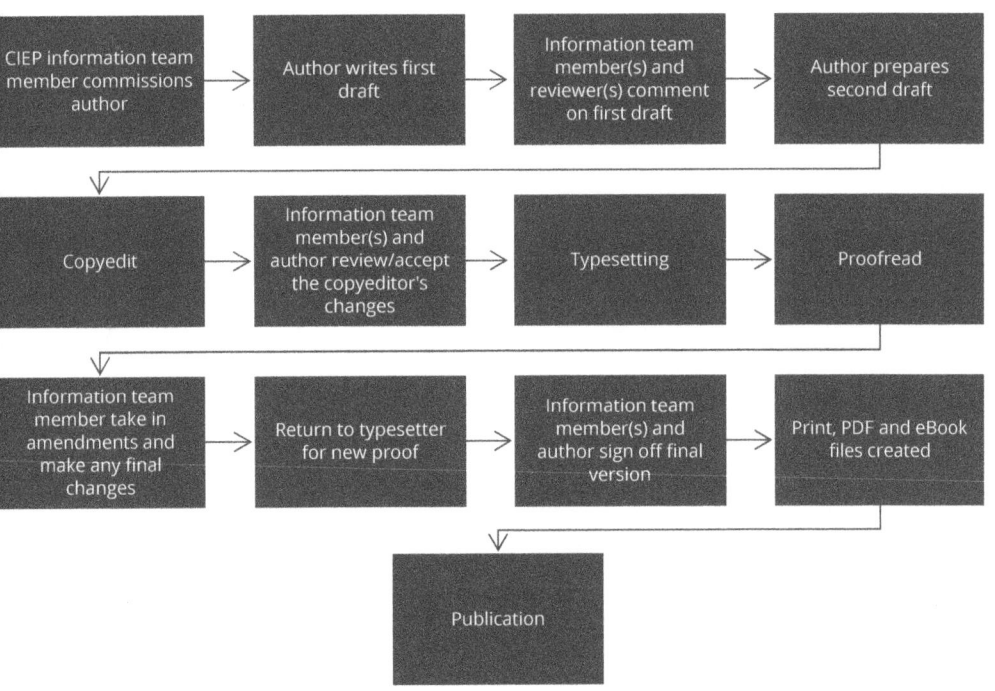

Figure 1: Example workflow for the publication of a CIEP guide

to start. When reading this guide, and throughout your editorial project management work, it is essential to remember that no two projects are the same; knowledge and experience will help you to adapt to different requirements and approaches.

If you're unsure in which order tasks should be completed, the CIEP has produced an infographic giving an **overview of a publishing workflow** (alongside other fact sheets for anyone who wants to know more about editing and proofreading).

5 | Scheduling

Editorial project management involves keeping a project on schedule – and that means ensuring that other people keep to the schedule too. It also requires an understanding of why there is a schedule, how it was created and who is responsible for any changes.

Publishing schedules are there to ensure that the final product is ready by the publication date. That publication date won't be chosen at random – it might tie in with an event, with a specific celebration, with the new academic year, with the end of the organisation's financial year, or similar.

A publishing schedule will be worked back from that date – whoever is creating the schedule has to understand the workflow and processes involved so that the schedule fits in the time available and is achievable.

Critical paths

Each task required for a project takes time – and adding up the time necessary for all tasks can provide a broad idea of how long a whole project will take. Some tasks are dependent on others – text cannot be proofread until there are proofs – and some tasks can be completed alongside others (see **Subsidiary critical paths**).

Schedules are based on the critical path of a project – the sequence of events or tasks that determines the shortest amount of time required to complete the project – to deliver the finished product. As each task in a critical path is dependent on its predecessor(s), a delay to any task impacts on those tasks that follow.

Taking the workflow in Figure 1 as an example, the table in Figure 2 on page 14 details the time taken (in working days) for the production of a CIEP guide.

Task	Time required
Commission	10 days
Write 1st draft	30 days
Review	10 days
Prepare 2nd draft	5 days
Copyedit	10 days
Review	2 days
Typesetting	5 days
Proofread	5 days
Final changes, sign-off and files	3 days
Online publication; printing and delivery	5 days
Total	**85 days**

Figure 2: Example of time taken to complete different tasks when publishing a CIEP guide

All of these tasks have to happen in sequence – none can happen before the previous one is complete – so the critical path runs from 'Commission', down through each task in the table to 'Online publication; printing and delivery'. Knowing that, we can work out the shortest time the project will take: 85 (working) days.

Subsidiary critical paths

Bigger projects may have subsidiary critical paths: if there are artworks to create or permissions to gather, these can happen alongside the copyediting and typesetting – some permissions may take months to be confirmed. Because of that, the production process splits, with a subsidiary critical path carrying on alongside the main critical path.

Things to consider when creating a schedule

In an ideal world, a new CIEP guide would take 85 working days (so 17 weeks) from start to finish. But even the CIEP does not exist in an ideal world, so other factors have to be considered when putting together a schedule:

- **The end product:** If it's a single book, a linear schedule will be suitable; a series of books may need a series of schedules; an online interactive resource could have a circular testing schedule (where the initial product is constantly revised in iterations based on feedback at reviewing stages, and even after it is released if customers encounter issues).
- **Blended products:** Print and digital elements may need to be published at the same time, or publication may be staggered.
- **Milestones and deadlines:** Significant moments in a project (milestones) may be more flexible than its final deadline.
- **Key dates and events:** When the content is due to be published is the most common driving factor behind schedules; other dates to bear in mind could be an author's or other stakeholder's holiday, or national holidays (especially if you and the supplier are in different time zones); the marketing team may need a proof copy for a book fair or conference.
- **Time zones:** If team members are spread across the globe, bear in mind that task deadlines may look different for different people. Your own end-of-day may be at a very different time to someone else's. Tasks allocated to these team members will need to reflect this – for instance, don't schedule someone to quickly cross-check a set of proofs within a day of the proofread if the original proofreader is in a time zone eight hours behind the cross-checker! Scheduling a regular meeting that everyone can attend may be challenging for the same reason.

Dependencies

Dependencies show the relationships between tasks and determine the order in which those tasks must happen.

In editorial project management, most dependencies are finish-to-start dependencies, where one task must finish before the next can start (see **Critical paths**).

There are also dependencies relating to people: do you need to finish the collation of proofs for a different project before you can prepare the files for the copyeditor on this project? If there's only one suitable specialist copyeditor, when are they available?

Variables

It's impossible to identify and deal with all variables on a project when the schedule is being put together, but being aware of and open to them now may well mitigate later issues. Think about time zones, technology, working with new suppliers, adapting to new ways of working, summer holidays ...

Contingency

If possible, leave space in the schedule for the unknown – at various points throughout or as a buffer at the end. If there isn't space for contingency, look at whether any tasks can be combined (such as development editing and copyediting) or streamlined. A project that starts with a tight schedule is at high risk of not going to plan.

Be realistic

Be honest about how long it takes for things to get done (well) – if you don't know how long something will take, ask someone who does. Base your schedule on giving everyone involved the time they need to complete the job to the quality expected within standard working hours.

Agile scheduling

Agile scheduling originates from agile software development and is not deadline based; doing regular reviews throughout a project means the schedule evolves as required. You may come across some editorial projects that use agile techniques alongside a fixed publication deadline. Agile scheduling is based on the principle of an ideal hour – see the **Resources** section of this guide for some suggestions of where you can find out more.

Scheduling tools and presentation

How a schedule looks matters. All stakeholders and suppliers must be able to see what is happening when. Schedules must be clear, concise and consistent. They shouldn't be bulked out with notes or instructions, which can be provided to only the people who need them via other means.

Schedules can be presented in a wide variety of ways – from a doodle on a scrap of paper to a detailed Microsoft Project file.

Visualisation, such as that used in Gantt charts (see Figure 3), is a great way to show how the project will work, and where the dependencies lie.

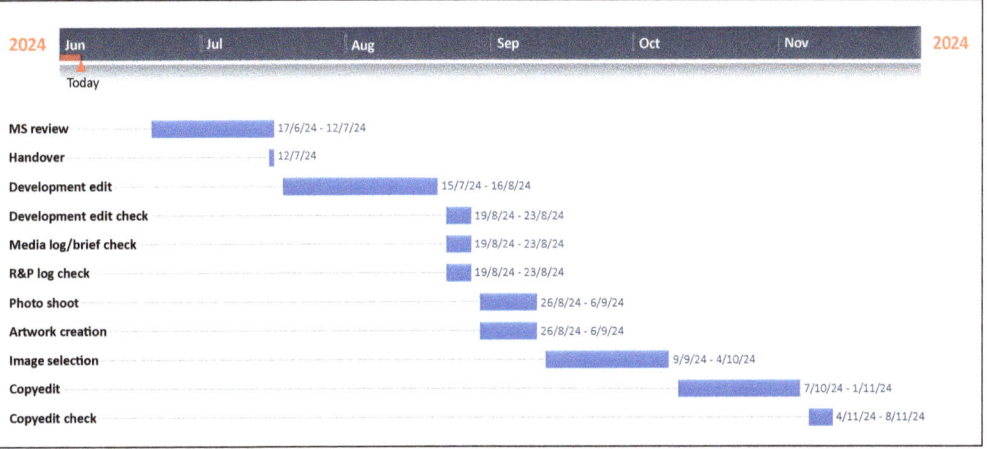

Figure 3: Example of a Gantt chart

Most clients and employers have preferred scheduling tools, but it's worth investigating the following:

- **Microsoft Project:** A heavy-duty project management tool, which does so much more than scheduling.
- **Microsoft Excel:** Most people are familiar with how Excel spreadsheets work – to make the most of its scheduling abilities, consider downloading Gantt chart templates and get to grips with formulas and functions (=TODAY(), which will give you the current date, and =WORKDAY, which excludes weekends and public holidays from the days counted, will save you hours of head scratching).
- **Microsoft Word:** This doesn't have the functionality of the other two Microsoft options, but can be used to show simple, clear schedules.
- **Online scheduling tools:** There are plenty out there, with three of the most popular being **Smartsheet**, **Asana** and **Basecamp** (which also has file-sharing capabilities).

Not all editorial project managers will be expected to create the schedule from scratch or even have input into its creation – your job might be simply to monitor the schedule, keep it updated and make sure everything is on track. However, sometimes you might be expected to create the schedule yourself, so it's worth being aware of how to do so and what a good schedule looks like.

Project update meetings will often refer to the RAG status of the schedule, or of the project as a whole. Green means that you are on, or ahead of, schedule. Amber indicates that most elements of the project are on schedule, but some are at risk of slipping or have already slipped a little. A red status is used to flag significant scheduling issues, with critical components missing, or at risk of missing, key deadlines. You will have to come up with strategic and creative solutions to bring a red project schedule back to green.

Managing a schedule

Whatever role you're currently in, you are used to managing your own schedule. You know the importance of prioritising and completing tasks in the time available. Managing the schedules for projects is the same – just with the added complexity of other people and external constraints. An editorial project manager must keep everyone on track, and deal effectively and efficiently with any issues.

Communication

The person with overall responsibility for the schedules needs to tell stakeholders and the editorial project manager what the key drivers are behind that schedule – and explain the protocol for requesting or making changes.

As editorial project manager, you must be clear and consistent about the schedule, informing suppliers about milestones and deadlines from the outset – and reminding them when handing over a task. Keep your team informed of any changes, and encourage them to be honest with you about any issues.

If team members or suppliers know who to talk to about potential problems, a solution can be enacted quickly.

Workflow

Use the schedule alongside the workflow (see **What is a project?**) – the workflow acts as a reminder about dependencies and concurrencies, and about what happens at each stage. If your client or employer doesn't have a formal workflow document, consider creating one.

Version control

Which version of the schedule is up to date? How do you know? Online tools, such as those listed earlier, will always show the most recent version, but static files on a server or in cloud storage may make it harder to identify the current schedule. A clear file-naming convention could be implemented, or changes could only be allowed by one person (such as the editorial project manager).

If any changes are made, ensure those who need to know about those changes are told as soon as possible.

Monitoring

Refer to the schedule regularly so that you know what should be happening when, and so that you can check in with, or chase, suppliers or colleagues.

Do opt for regular catch-up meetings with stakeholders – they are a great way to keep on top of the schedule, and to build relationships – and send an occasional email to suppliers to see how things are progressing. Again, keep the communication lines open so that issues are identified and addressed quickly.

Kanban boards are a popular tool, providing a visual representation of where the project and tasks within the project are right now – this could be sticky notes on a wall, or a collaborative online tool (**Trello** seems to be the most widely used, and **Asana** also has these capabilities). They are also commonly used to gather ideas for, or at, project retrospective meetings.

Dealing with the unexpected

Unexpected issues tend to originate from common sources:

- **People**: accident, bereavement, illness, time management, having the wrong skillset
- **Technical**: computer or server downtime, unexpected internet issues, out-of-date software, accessing online resources (including setting up relevant accounts access, passwords and so on for external team members such as freelancers)
- **Content**: permissions refused, poor quality, inappropriate, something is missing
- **World**: those so-called acts of God, changes of government and/or policy.

When a delay seems likely, find out the cause – and, with the relevant colleagues or suppliers, work out how to either stop the delay or limit its impact. It may be time to use some of that contingency, or to streamline tasks later in the process.

Major complications need immediate escalation (they must be reported to the product owner). They may result in the whole project being put on hold – that is a decision for the product owner to make but do offer constructive suggestions.

Whatever issues you face, note them down ready for a review at the end of the project, for your own development and to provide feedback to suppliers or the product owner.

Implications

The effects of a delay or change of schedule depend on the nature of the project, and on the solution chosen. For any schedule change, the possible and definite implications need to be reviewed:

- Is the change/solution going to push the task over its allotted budget?
- Does the solution risk missed sales?
- Will a later publication date mean the product misses a key event/date?

- Is there adequate time contingency?
- Will the change/solution have further implications later in the project?
- Will the suppliers still be available?
- Will you still be available?
- Are there any legal consequences?

Scheduling your own time

As well as managing a project's schedule, you need to manage your own time and commitments. This is a skill for which time-management webinars, books and workshops can only scratch the surface – experience will tell you how long it takes to, for example, collate comments from five reviewers, track down an available specialist editor or proofreader willing to work within the budget available, or upload files to a client's bespoke cloud storage.

For all projects, keep a record of how much time you spend doing each task to build up an informed picture of what future projects may involve.

Be realistic – and honest – about how many hours there are in your day. Sometimes, schedule pressures will mean that you have to stretch your limits, but if those limits are constantly being stretched, talk to your client before it affects the quality of your work.

6 | Briefing

Briefing is key to a project – a brief tells someone what they are required to do (possibly how) and by when.

You will receive a brief when you agree to take on a project, and you will then have to provide briefs to those you commission to undertake specific tasks during the project. Your brief may be in the form of a phone call, a thread of emails, a kick-off meeting, a written document, handover notes from a previous project manager if you are taking over halfway through, or a combination of all or some of these.

The quality of a brief can determine the success of a project: if someone is unclear about what they are supposed to do, they may not do what you need them to.

Understanding the client's brief

The editorial project manager's role in a project begins once they receive their brief – in whatever form it comes. Take notes, ask questions, get confirmation, check any contradictions or gaps.

Before starting a project, you must know:

- what the end product is
- what your tasks and responsibilities are
- what the workflow is
- who should deliver what, and when
- what you must deliver, and when
- what the budget is
- who your contacts are, and how to get in touch with them.

The person handing the project over to you may also give you relevant documentation, samples, templates and login details for any project management/scheduling/content management websites or systems.

Read everything you have been given and any notes you have taken, and make sure you can access any relevant systems, then ask any questions you have before the project starts. If you don't receive the documents, details or logins you're expecting, chase your client for them.

It's likely that something will come up during a project that you didn't think of in the early stages – or it may contradict what you've been told before – address those questions or issues as soon as they arise. Don't make assumptions about what the client wants or what the project needs.

Briefing your team

You've no doubt had a piece of work thrown at you and been told to get on with it. That's not a good brief. A brief explains what needs to be done, by when, to what standard and for what cost. Use your knowledge and experience of good, and bad, briefs when preparing them for the people you want to work on your projects.

If you have been briefed properly, you will have a clear idea of who you are going to commission (on some projects, all or some commissions may have already been made), and what you need them to do. You may have to brief people who know the processes well, or external suppliers who need a more detailed breakdown of what is required. Each project will require different things of you, and those you work with; you may be provided with brief templates the client requires you to use, or you could use briefs you have received or been given on other projects as a starting point.

Ensure that you create **SMART** briefs: Specific, Measurable, Attainable, Relevant and Time specific.

- A brief must be **specific** to the task and to the person who will carry out the task: it should cover what the project is, what their role is, what the task is and what their objectives are.
- **Measurable**. Define the scope of the task, the deliverables and the deadlines.
- Make sure what you are asking for is **attainable** and tell the supplier to get in touch if something is or becomes unattainable.

- Give your supplier the **relevant** information for them to be able to do the work to the quality you require, in the time available. Avoid information overload. Ask if there's anything else they need to know.
- **Time specific**. Tell them what the deadline is, and if there are any milestones they need to hit.

Briefing a wide range of suppliers and team members

You won't know the precise details of what everyone involved in the publishing process does – and you don't need to. However, you must brief them effectively to keep the project on track. Draw on your own experiences, knowledge and common sense. Learn from those who have already worked on the project – designs, templates or digital platforms may already be in place.

Always be open to questions about the briefs you have created, and answer those questions as quickly as you can. Acknowledge the question if it's going to take a while to find out the answer. Getting the lines of communication open now will make communication easier further down the line.

7 | Budgeting

As an editorial project manager, you probably won't be involved in drawing up the budget for a project. It's likely you'll be given details of the expected costings for each element of the publication process as part of your briefing. You will need to adhere to the budget you are given, and, as ever, flag up any concerns or issues as soon as they arise.

Setting the budget

The size and scope of a budget is very much linked to three things: cost, time and quality. The product owner will know which of these elements is the most important with regard to a specific project – they may want to spend more money to get the highest-quality product, or they may want something as soon as possible. If time is the main priority, then costs may need to be higher; if costs have to stay low, then schedule slips and delays may not be of concern.

You may be given a set budget for the whole project, or a breakdown for each section of work. Occasionally, you may be faced with quoting for a project as part of the initial planning stage, so you'll need to research which suppliers you might use in bringing that quote together. (And don't forget to include your own fee in that quote, and some contingency.) The time/cost/quality triangle is commonly evoked in project management – in almost all projects, you can have two sides of the triangle (such as more time and higher quality) but at the expense of the third (such as a higher cost).

Negotiating your fee

A client may come to you with a project management budget in mind, or may ask you what your rates are. Consider your fee closely, bearing in mind the breadth, complexity and timescales of the project. Discuss with the client who will be responsible for paying external suppliers and how

7 | Budgeting

that payment process will work. If the client wants you to make those payments, get quotes from suppliers. Invest time in ensuring that the budget will work for you and your suppliers, and that the client's payment schedule won't leave you with cashflow problems.

During the project, if you can see that the fee you have agreed isn't going to cover all the work involved (especially if there has been scope creep), get in touch with the client and make suggestions about how to go forward. You may suggest that they pay you more, but you could also consider asking for in-house assistance, or a change to the workflow or responsibilities.

Types of fee

Hourly
Some budgets will be based on hourly fees for certain (or all) suppliers. This type of fee is falling out of favour in some organisations given the unpredictability of the final figure. If using hourly fees, give a supplier a maximum number of hours they can claim for (and tell them to inform

you as soon as possible if that maximum proves to be unrealistic). If you don't know how long a specific piece of work will take, ask potential suppliers for an estimate.

Fixed fee
Some clients may require you, and your suppliers, to work for fixed fees. These fees may be based on a page rate, or the estimated time a project/task will take. Using fixed fees lowers the risk of costs going beyond an acceptable level for a project; however, the time/extent estimates may turn out not to reflect the actual amount of work required. A client may make any contingency or leeway clear when briefing you on the budget, but you should discuss increased costs with the client as soon as concerns arise. If needs be, halt a supplier's work on the project until revised fees (or alternative options) are agreed.

Rate cards
Some publishers or organisations use rate cards – the fees they will pay – for common editorial and production tasks, and will agree these with any project manager (or project management company) that they use on a regular basis. The rates given on the rate card form the basis for the fees for the project. However, it's always worth negotiating with suppliers to keep costs down, rather than just offering the given rate.

Task	Rate per page (based on planned extent)
Project management	£7.50
Development edit	£7.50
Copyedit	£5.25
Proofread	£3.25
Index	£3.00
Fact-check	£2.75
Answer-check	£2.75

Figure 4: Example of basic rate card (rates given are for illustration purposes only)

Rate cards may also include fees for picture research and use of images, artwork, permissions, typesetting, specialist reviews, native speaker checks, and testing for digital products.

Contingency

Establish at the start of the project what contingency there is within the client's budget, and also within your own. If you will be paying suppliers directly, consider what you are being paid in relation to what you are going to have to pay out.

It is also worth confirming whether you can move money from one part of the budget to another – if the copyedit comes in under budget, can you move the remaining money to cover unexpected illustration costs?

Managing the budget

Communicating, recording and reporting

As a project progresses, you will need to regularly report on what fees have been agreed, invoiced for and paid. A client/employer may have a specific form or spreadsheet for you to complete or keep updated – ensure you do so promptly and accurately. If they do not have a required format, provide the figures in a clear format – Excel is useful for budget reports given its accessible tools for formulas.

Budget reports will be made to specific timelines, depending on the project. Reports can be weekly, monthly or tied to project milestones (end of first proofs, end of final proofs ...). Try to keep your figures up to date at all times, but make sure you are aware of the reporting dates so, at a minimum, figures can be updated ahead of time for each report. Reports must be dated and saved under a unique file name, unless they are collected in an online tool such as Smartsheet or Microsoft Project. Careful record-keeping can be crucial if any disputes or issues arise.

You may decide to collect more information on expenditure for your own, or for your project management company's, records. Again, ensure the records you keep are clear; add notes if necessary to help others who may look at the figures.

Monitoring

Budget reports are also useful for monitoring costs, and keeping track of whether contingencies have been used or overspends have been covered by a different part of the budget.

If there are overspends, keep a record of what caused them and use those notes during the project retrospective meeting.

Bear in mind that the fee you offer a supplier may differ from the cost to the client (if you are working via a packager – see **Working for a project management company**). Make sure you know what you have charged and what you have paid, and double-check the figures in any correspondence with suppliers or reports to clients.

Escalation

Any increase in costs must be taken back to the client as soon as possible – otherwise there is a risk that they will not cover that increase and you will have to find the money from elsewhere (including possibly your own fee). Be prepared when going back to the client: understand why the cost does not match the estimate and consider any possible ways to reduce other costs.

As ever, early communication is preferable to an apology after an overspend. Additional spending may need to be signed off – which may take time – and work on a project may need to be halted while budgets are revised and agreed. This may affect the schedule so be aware of the implications and inform those who need to know.

Change requests
Change requests relate to changes to a project requested by the client, such as changing black and white figures to colour or adding in an additional proof stage. These changes fall outside the scope of the original project so additional costs should be agreed before the changes are actioned.

Such changes could be seen as routine corrections – this is where scope creep can occur – but review each alteration and its related costs as they arise, and communicate with the client if scope creep appears, especially if it affects costs.

Purchase orders
Purchase orders (POs), or work orders, are legally binding documents that indicate an intention to buy goods or services at an agreed price. POs are compulsory within some organisations, and payment will not be made without a PO reference on an invoice. In these instances, ensure that you receive a PO for the work that you are undertaking, and that you provide POs to all individuals and companies you commission. Work on a task should not start until a PO has been raised and sent to the person commissioned.

If you are required to raise POs on a project, you will need access to the appropriate company financial system if there is one in place. You will also need training to use the system and raise POs correctly, so it's a good idea to bring this up early with your client to ensure this is set up as soon as possible.

8 | Management and communication

The previous few chapters have looked at some of the bigger tasks involved in editorial project management: this one considers the softer skills that permeate a whole project.

Selecting the right people

It is unlikely that, as an editorial project manager, you will have to choose all the people who work on a project. You can choose whether to work for a specific company, but you won't have influence over which employees from that company will work on a project; depending on your remit for a project, you may be able to choose external suppliers (such as copyeditors, proofreaders, fact-checkers, typesetters or indexers). However people are selected for a project, you will need to manage relationships and communicate effectively.

Editorial specialists

You are much more likely to be involved in selecting editorial suppliers – and who to choose will depend on the project. You may opt for someone you've worked with before, someone recommended by a trusted colleague or collaborator, someone your client has on their books, or someone you have found via an online directory (for instance, the CIEP's **Directory of Editorial Services** and the Society of Indexers' **Directory of Professional Indexers**).

Wherever you find a potential supplier, check that they are experienced in the subject matter, have undertaken training and CPD, and have worked on similar projects. If you contract someone with little or no experience, do check that they understand your brief and regularly check in with them to discuss how things are going.

Some editorial freelancers are able to fill their schedules weeks, or even months, in advance so you may have to act quickly to get the person you want. Give them enough relevant information about the project for them to be able to accurately assess if the work is viable for them.

Tell them:

- the task involved
- a little bit about the content (format, audience)
- the extent of the work (eg word count, page extent, number of images/figures)
- the deadline, and any milestones
- the budget.

It's up to you whether you approach more than one person at the same time, or whether you wait to hear back from one before approaching another. Do you need to get someone on board quickly? What would you do if two people said yes to the work? You could consider giving a deadline for a response if you need to hear back quickly.

Technical specialists

It's common for technical suppliers, such as digital specialists and typesetters, to be decided by the product owner, or other teams within an organisation. However, you will still need to build effective relationships and keep the lines of communication open throughout a project, and be ready to deal with any issues that arise.

The editorial project manager

The client chose *you* to work on their project. Keep in mind the qualities and skills you bring with you. You might not be an expert in every stage of the publishing process, but you can understand what needs to happen when, ask questions to deepen that understanding, be honest if something goes wrong (or could be about to go wrong), suggest solutions to problems and assess how things are going.

Working with your client

Publishing projects can have a very different set-up, depending on the client. You might find that you work closely with an in-house project manager, who is sometimes your sole contact within the organisation. Alternatively, you might be part of a large in-house team and be expected to communicate with numerous people across a wide variety of teams. Make sure you are aware of the main contact on each team, and broadly understand what their job role entails and where they fit in. However the project communication channels are set up, remember to be pleasant and professional to everyone involved, and value every person's contribution. When problems arise, it can be tempting to side with the teams or individuals you have the most contact with, but others who may seem further removed from the project will often have relevant information or raise points you haven't considered. Large organisations can sometimes engender a political environment on difficult projects, with different teams having their own priorities. Remain as impartial as possible, gather facts objectively and escalate as necessary in order to ensure the best decisions for the project are reached.

Reporting and feedback

During a project, reporting and feedback are key processes that need to be undertaken in a timely and efficient fashion.

Reporting

You will need to report specific information to the client – they should cover this in your brief or during the handover meeting. If you're not sure, ask. They may want this information in a weekly email, during a daily/weekly/fortnightly meeting, or in a monthly spreadsheet. If you think that there is other information they need to know, highlight why you think it will be of use to them. Part of your job is to filter everything that's going on and send the right info to the right people. You will learn through doing, and through working with specific people, and you may want to change how you do things as a project progresses.

Establish early on who you should contact about which things: who is the first point of contact for budgeting? Who needs to know about scheduling changes?

Feedback

Providing constructive feedback takes thought and effort, but it enables all parties to see where improvements can be made and gives an opportunity to praise work done well.

You need to give feedback to:

- the client
- your editorial suppliers
- the technical specialists.

There may be a formal feedback mechanism in place with a client – possibly in the form of a retrospective meeting at the end of a project. Throughout a project, do keep notes about what is going well and what

could be improved in a similar project. Don't assume you'll remember at the end of a project, especially if it's one with a long timescale.

You may not be able to give feedback directly to technical specialists, but still do so via the client. It's likely you'll be the only point of contact for an external editorial supplier, so offer timely feedback as soon as you have checked their work. It may be that you provide additional feedback further down the line (such as to a copyeditor after the content has been proofread).

When giving feedback to anyone involved in a project:

- be honest with yourself and those you are working with
- don't play the blame game
- explain the wider implications of a decision/mistake/action
- make it a learning opportunity for all involved
- don't make it personal
- explain how things could have been done differently, and what can be learned from the experience
- be professional
- don't forget the good stuff – give praise where praise is due.

Keep calm and carry on

Each project will present you with different issues and problems, sometimes those that you couldn't have predicted or imagined. Just as when providing feedback to others, don't get personal about your own performance. You will make a mistake. So will someone else you're working with.

The skill in these situations is to admit, accept, rectify and move on. Dwelling on how you (or a colleague) 'should' have done something differently isn't good for you and it isn't good for the project.

If faced with criticism, be reasonable, be objective, be calm and be proactive. If needs be, take a step back, count to ten, go for a walk, have a cup of tea – whatever you need to do to rein in your emotions and bring professionalism back to the fore.

8 | Management and communication

All that said, if your involvement in a project becomes untenable because of the behaviour of others or the demands on your time (or sanity), think about what would need to change to enable you to carry on. Talk to your client – and, again, be honest.

Sometimes you may have to work in a way you don't like, with people you don't like, because of a client's demands or requirements. Remember that projects are finite – this one will end! And you can use the experience to inform how you work and what you work on in future.

9 | Working for a project management company

Rather than working directly for a publisher, you may be offered editorial project management work via a project management (PM) company or packager. These companies run projects end-to-end on behalf of publishing clients, and are commonly used by many publishing houses. This adds in another layer between you and the publishing organisation, which can also mean added layers of complexity. The other chapters in this guide are all still relevant to working with a PM company, but this section offers some specifics to keep in mind when you accept a job with a packager.

Project set up

Different PM companies have differing preferred ways of working. You might operate as a contractor using your own email address, but some companies will give you a company email address and access to their remote desktop for the duration of the project. Having direct access to project systems in this way can be a real advantage and make you feel truly part of the team. Make sure you establish how you are expected to work alongside the packager at the outset of the project, if it's not already clear from the brief.

Communication

When working for a PM company, you should always bear in mind that you are representing them to the end client, in much the same way as you represent yourself directly to clients. Remain polite and professional – even if you disagree at times with decisions made by the PM company. Typically, communication with the end client will go via an in-house project manager at the packager, but you will likely still have plenty of direct contact with the client, including in team meetings and via email. Some packagers have templates that you can use for common tasks, such as handover emails. Always run any decisions past your in-house contact at the PM company and get approval *before* communicating them to the end client. It is key to ensure you and the packager have a similar understanding of the project at all times.

Schedule

You will likely not have a choice regarding the software you use for scheduling. The PM company will have to adhere to the preferences of the end client – this means they may not have direct experience of working with the chosen tool themselves, unless they have worked with the client before. If you are unsure how to use the tool provided, ask the packager to provide training or request it directly from the client – this will make everyone's lives easier down the line.

Budget

The PM company will take a small percentage of the fee for each task – for example, if they are being paid £7.50 per page for project management, you might receive £6 per page. However, some companies will only work with other companies rather than directly with freelances, so if you are a sole trader, being sub-contracted by a PM company may widen your opportunities and experience. As ever, for every project you need to assess its financial viability for your business.

Budgets on packaged projects are often very tight, so you should be prepared to negotiate with external suppliers in order to get the best possible rates for the project.

10 | Being an editorial project manager

Previous chapters have told you what editorial projects look like, how they can be managed and what skills you will need. But away from the processes, timelines, tools and bottom lines, what is the life of an editorial project manager like? How can you be the best project manager you can be?

Communication

Throughout this guide, communication has come up over and over again – this really is the key to successful editorial project management. Without clear, respectful communication, a project is destined to get messy.

Be professional, calm and cooperative. Don't assign blame if issues arise; take a positive step forward to keep things moving. If you make a mistake, admit it, apologise for it, then take that positive step and get it all back on track. Thank people for the work they do, and acknowledge work done well.

If you've worked as a freelance copyeditor or proofreader for a while, you may be out of the habit of talking face-to-face, but most situations are most easily resolved in person or (more likely) via a video call. You're going to need to work on using your voice and the technology – so get practising! Your client's communication preferences may not match your own.

Project teams are increasingly spread out geographically, so many projects will require the project manager to chair regular team meetings via video call. This can be intimidating at first – ensure you understand your client's requirements for meetings. Do they have a particular template or agenda they'd like you to follow, for example, a schedule update followed by a budget discussion with general concerns raised at the end? Are there specific documents that must be referred to during the meetings, such as the live schedule, a change request tracker, an issue log or similar? Setting expectations will ensure you can prepare for the meetings in advance and deliver them to the client's satisfaction.

Get familiar with the different tools available within the video conferencing system. Most have features such as muting individual or all participants, screen sharing, recording the call, raising hands, break-out rooms where people can have smaller group discussions, sections for comments or notes, and so on. Make sure you include the cost of preparation and delivery time for meetings in your rates, as they can take up a surprisingly large amount of your time. Even if you are not chairing the meeting, remember that attending a meeting forms part of your billable hours (if you are being paid on a time basis).

Remember: communication is as much about listening as it is about talking.

Be human

Be interested in the people you are working with, and get an idea of what other commitments they are managing. Be understanding. This will help you get the best from them, and can build up a longer-term working relationship.

Lessons learned

At the end of a task, and at the end of a project, reflect on what worked and what didn't. Keep a log of what you'd do again, and what you need to steer clear of or do differently.

A retrospective meeting with the product owner or wider team is the perfect forum for discussing the highs and lows. Be honest with yourself and with your client – steer clear of a blame game.

Even if there is no retrospective meeting with your client, have one with yourself to remind you of your strengths and to highlight where you can develop further.

Managing expectations

When starting a project, listen. Understand what your client/employer is expecting from you. Be honest if there is something that is out of your comfort zone, or you are unable to do (such as a 6pm meeting every Tuesday when you already have other commitments). Likewise, be clear about what you are asking colleagues or suppliers to do. If you can see ambiguity or confusion, deal with it there and then.

Keeping in touch

During the project, keep in touch with your client/employer, the product owner, colleagues, suppliers – and tell them how they can contact you.

If anyone sends you files, invoices or information, reply and acknowledge receipt – and encourage your suppliers to do the same.

Managing your own time

This was covered in the **Scheduling** section. It isn't a skill that comes easily, and it takes a lot of practice, and trial and error. Poor time management can lead to poor-quality work and mistakes, which then can have time and/or cost implications later on. Just like any other skill, time management improves with experience and awareness.

Acknowledge and respect your limits, and ask for support if you need it.

Keeping records

Keep records about every project you work on. This information may be needed by you, by your client, by those who help you run your business or by those who assess your business (like the tax authority).

For each project, record:

- the client's details
- the project's title (and ISBN/ISSN where relevant)
- the start date
- the publication date
- the estimated hours you will spend on the project

- the actual numbers you spent on the project (and what those hours were spent doing)
- the fee (and whether it's hourly, fixed or per page)
- the details of your invoices, and of any suppliers' invoices
- who you have commissioned to work on the project (and what they have been commissioned to do, when and for how much).

How you record these details (and any others) is down to personal preference – a spreadsheet, a notebook, in an app. You may need to add your hours worked to a timesheet; do check that the hours on your invoice(s) tally with those in the timesheet. You can use an app such as **Toggl** to track your time if needed.

File storage and distribution

If you are working on any project over 50 pages, or with illustrations and images, you are going to have a lot of large files to store. You must store those files safely and securely, and organise them in such a way that others can easily find what they need.

Files may be stored on a specific server, in a content management system (such as **SharePoint**) or in cloud storage (such as **Dropbox** or **OneDrive**). Some clients may even have a virtual desktop in place to allow you access to their main systems. Get to grips with whatever system is being used as quickly as possible so that you can explain it to suppliers if/when necessary.

It makes sense to also store key files locally (on your computer) in case you cannot access internet-based storage, if you are permitted to do so. However, some clients may have strict measures surrounding security or confidentiality, and will not allow personal file storage. Check your contract carefully for expectations surrounding intellectual property rights and data protection.

Back up your files. It doesn't matter how – automatically, manually – but do it.

Building up and using the experience

Reading this guide alone won't make you an editorial project manager. If what you've read here has spiked your interest, consider taking a training course – the CIEP's online **Editorial Project Management** course has a similar structure to this guide and uses case studies and exercises to get you thinking like an editorial project manager. The **Resources** section of this guide gives suggestions for further reading.

If you already work in publishing, talk to your clients or colleagues about their management tools, processes and workflow. What do they look for in a project manager? What do their project managers need to know?

Practices and methodologies change and adapt all the time. Be open to change and new ideas. Seek out appropriate training courses, relevant books or blogs, talk to other editorial project managers – not just when you're starting out, but throughout your career. There is always something more to learn.

11 | Resources

Books

Editorial Project Management by Barbara Horn, Horn Editorial Books, 2006.

This is currently the only book available specifically on editorial project management and it is now out of print, although it is possible to source used copies online or from other editors. Technologies have moved on substantially since its publication in 2006, but it covers the key principles and gives plenty of examples and exercises across the whole publication process.

Project Management: Absolute Beginner's Guide by Gregory M. Horine, Que Publishing, 2022.

Now in its fifth edition, this book covers the basics of project management from a general perspective and includes advice on preparing for the PMP certification. It is not specific to the publishing industry.

Blogs

At the time of writing, there are posts about editorial project management on the **CIEP blog**, for example:

https://blog.ciep.uk/editorial-project-management/
https://blog.ciep.uk/editorial-project-manager/
https://blog.ciep.uk/editorial-project-management-teams/

Hazel Bird shares her experiences and advice on her **Wordstitch blog**.

BookMachine organises networking events for people working in the publishing industry; on its website, the **editorial channel** has articles of relevance to editorial project management – and it's worth having a browse through the other channels too.

It's also worth browsing the **Publishing Training Centre's blog**.

Courses

At the time of writing, the CIEP offers an online course in **Editorial Project Management**.

The Publishing Training Centre (PTC) has relevant **courses** which are currently taught online.

Project management

There are thousands of books available on general project management techniques and approaches – as well as acres of online content.

The **Association for Project Management** (APM) provides a wide range of resources and information, as well as training aimed at different levels of experience.

PRINCE2 is a popular project management certification, but bear in mind that it consists of a specific methodology for running projects. Therefore, its main relevance is if you are working with organisations that specifically use PRINCE2, which isn't the case in most editorial contexts.

Keep in mind that you may only come across many of these approaches briefly or to a limited extent in an editorial context. Nevertheless, get searching and get reading!

Agile project management

The agile project management methodology originated in software development, but aspects are now being used in many other fields, including publishing. The **APM website** covers agile in depth; there are also helpful summaries and guides by **CIO** and on **Stackify**.

About the authors

Abi Saffrey has worked on and managed editorial projects since she started out as an editorial assistant in 2000. After nine years working for publishers, business information providers and quangos, she started her own editorial business and now focuses on project management and copyediting.

Emily Kopieczek has been in the field of editorial project management for over a decade. She worked in-house for two publishers from 2012 to 2019, culminating as a Senior Managing Editor. She now runs a business providing editorial services for the ELT sector, specialising in project management, copyediting, proofreading and digital reviews. She holds the APM PMQ.

editsbyemily.com

Acknowledgements

I am grateful to my previous employers, and past and present clients, for introducing me to and inspiring my interest in editorial project management – and for showing me how it should (and occasionally how it shouldn't) be done. Thanks also to the CIEP and the PTC for the many CPD opportunities over the past 14 years, and to Tracey Cowell (**passionforpublishing.co.uk**), Wendy Toole (**wendytoole.com**) and Mary Hobbins (**businessblend.info**) for their helpful comments on the draft of this guide.

Abi Saffrey

I want to thank the CIEP for giving me the opportunity to help update this guide. I'd like to echo Abi's sentiments regarding the CIEP's and PTC's CPD and training. Thanks also go to the APM, whose training and qualification have been invaluable. I'd especially like to thank all my amazing colleagues and clients from over the years, for making every project special and memorable in its own unique way!

Emily Kopieczek

www.ingramcontent.com/pod-product-compliance
Lightning Source LLC
Chambersburg PA
CBHW041315110526
44591CB00022B/2918